Worlds Beyond Words

True stories about the power of reading

Alison Stokes

ACCENT PRESS LTD

Contents

Acknowledgements

Thank you to all the people who have shared their stories and to NIACE Dysgu Cymru; Llamau, Cardiff; the Ministry of Defence and the Basic Skills Unit at the Welsh Assembly Government for their help in compiling this book.

Foreword

There is no doubt that learning to read and write has transformed my life and the lives of my children. It has also changed the fortunes of the people in this book.

There are many reasons why people leave school without basic reading skills, as these stories prove.

For some, like young father Edward John, it was a troubled childhood and being taken into care. Teenager Ruth Bond suffered mental illness as a schoolgirl and lost out on part of her education. For African refugee Lutala Kabe learning to read in English as a second language was a matter of life or death. Swansea City footballer Angel Rangel needed to learn to succeed on the pitch.

The stories of former steel-worker Joe Monks, Afghanistan war hero Jonathan Owen, teaching assistant Jill Jury and world-famous architect Lord Richard Rogers prove that you can be written off at school yet still make a success of your life. Their problems, like my own, stemmed from dyslexia.

Six years ago my literary skills were so bad that I couldn't even write a cheque or reply to an email. Reading a book would take months. I also had a very poor attention span and I struggled to concentrate on anything for more than a few minutes. This made life incredibly frustrating.

Although I wasn't diagnosed with dyslexia and dyspraxia until I was 21, learning difficulties had dominated my life. School was a nightmare and my poor concentration meant that it wasn't long before I began to fall behind. My teachers did everything they could to help me, but it seemed as if I had an inability to retain information. Even the basic things like copying from the blackboard were a struggle and in the end I spent most lessons staring out of the window, daydreaming.

After school, my career focused on rugby. Over the following years I played for Wales 52 times, captaining the side on seven occasions. I also played for the British Lions and the Barbarians.

Although I'm incredibly proud of what I achieved in my rugby career, the shadow of learning difficulties always hung over me. I remember once a middle-aged woman threw a carefully signed autograph back in my face because I'd spelt her name wrong – this sort of thing happened all the time.

On another occasion I remember driving my daughter Lucy to school. When we arrived at the gates she realised she had left her gym kit at home and knew she would get into trouble with the teacher. She asked me if I would write her a note. I'm ashamed to say I couldn't. I covered up. 'Go on, you'll be all right,' I told her. I left her at the school gates and I cried to myself on the way home. I was so ashamed. I had sent a six-year-old to have a row from her teacher just because I couldn't write.

The moment that my early learning difficulties really came back to haunt me was the moment when my wife and I had to face the fact that both our children were showing signs of learning difficulties.

My son Steele had terrible problems with his co-ordination and struggled to ride a bike even though all of his friends could. We later found out he had dyspraxia. Meanwhile my daughter Lucy had huge difficulty with reading and found school very frustrating, just as I had years earlier.

My life changed for the better when ex-Scotland international Kenny Logan introduced me to the Dore Programme, a new treatment for dyslexia. In January 2006 I was diagnosed as severely dyslexic and it turned out my problems were a lot worse than Lucy's or Steele's. As a family we followed the programme. For me it was incredible to realise I was finally winning the battle. My reading ability went through the roof and my concentration, which had always held me back, improved dramatically. Suddenly I was able to focus, which made communicating and expressing myself so much easier. It was as if someone had switched on a light bulb. I saw an improvement in my children, too. Their teachers were amazed by their progress. Steele's co-ordination improved so much that he was even able to ride a bike – which I'd never thought possible.

Today I am not only able to read and write but am able to do things I never thought would be possible. It feels like my world has opened up. Everything seems so much easier.

In 2007 I published *The Hardest Test* as part of the Quick Reads initiative. It told the story of my journey as I overcame my learning disabilities.

As a Quick Reads author I have been asked to speak at many events and have met many learners and their families. Their situations are often very different from mine, but many have the same problem: being ashamed to admit their problems.

The people in this book have taken those first steps to overcome their difficulties and should be proud of what they have achieved.

Their stories are an inspiration for others.

Scott Quinnell

A Spanish Swansea Jack

by Angel Rangel

When I came to Wales to play football for Swansea City I didn't speak a word of English. Off the pitch the only word I knew how to say was 'hello'. But soon I learned my first words on the pitch ... 'f*** off'.

I was twenty-four and playing for the Spanish side Terrassa FC in Barcelona when I got a telephone call from Roberto Martinez, who was Swansea City's manager at the time.

'Come and play for me at Swansea,' he said in Spanish. 'I have been keeping an eye on you and I think a move to Wales could improve your career.'

I knew of Martinez's reputation as a great manager. He had been a player in Spain who had made the move into football management and was now making a name for himself in the UK. To some of the Swansea fans he was 'God'. Martinez had visited Terrassa earlier in the season to watch another player. It just happened that on that day I played the best game of my career and he liked what he saw.

'I think you could be a great signing for Swansea,' Martinez continued, as if needing to convince me that a move to Wales would be a step up in my career. I needed no persuasion. At Terrassa I was playing semi-professional football; here was a chance to become a professional and play in the English League One. I booked my plane ticket to Wales.

There was only one problem: my English – or lack of it. I had grown up in Sant Carles de la Rapita in Tarragona, a small village south of Salou on the Costa Dorada in Spain, 2,000 miles away from Wales. There both my parents and my two sisters spoke Spanish. I had learnt English in the third year at school – but that was more than ten years ago, so my knowledge was very poor. I spoke a bit of Italian and Portuguese but couldn't speak a word of English and found it very difficult to communicate.

When I arrived in Swansea on 29 June 2007, everything was shocking. I had left Spain in the scorching sunshine, and in Swansea it was 'pissing down' with rain (a term I learnt very quickly). The food was different, too. I missed my mother's Spanish omelette. I had never heard of the 'The Full Monty' breakfast of bacon, eggs and sausage until I came to Swansea. I liked to start the day with something lighter, like a croissant or a sandwich. And the coffee was too strong. The other players would laugh at me because I needed to put eight sachets of sugar in my cup before I could drink it. Although it was a culture shock, the people were friendly and made me feel at home from day one – even if they couldn't understand a word I said.

For those first few weeks I didn't say a lot. There were so many words to learn. I bought myself a dictionary and kept it with me all the time. Every time I heard a new word I would go away and look up its meaning in the dictionary.

The other players and staff at Swansea City would laugh at me because I couldn't even say 'Good morning'. I just smiled and said 'Hello' and waved my arms around. It's surprising how much you can communicate by just using gestures.

Having Martinez as a manager and two Spanish team-mates – Guillem Bauza, who had also signed to Swansea City that season from Mallorca's Espanyol club, and Andrea Orlandi, who came from the club Deportivo Alaves – made things easier.

In the early days Martinez would give me instructions in Spanish. He also gave me a list of football terms which I had to learn on the pitch. Words like 'man on' which meant that someone was chasing you when you had the ball, or 'leave it' for times when the ball was going out and you shouldn't touch it. I also learned not to argue with the referee. He arranged for Bauza, Orlandi and myself to have English lessons. After a month I knew all the language on the pitch and quite a few swear words, too. Then I started to learn the language off the pitch.

We signed up with Kingsway College in Swansea and twice a week a tutor would come to the club and give us two-hour lessons in the boardroom. It was intense and I found it difficult. The writing was not too bad as I had managed that at school, but speaking was difficult.

Reading helped me a lot. The first books I read were children's fiction. My team-mate Bauza's English was better than mine and he was reading all the Harry Potter books. The first book I read was for young children, a book about knights. It was less than fifty pages long, but it took me more than a month to reach the end. Every other word I would have to stop and look up the meaning in my dictionary. It was slow progress but it was good practice for me to learn different types of words. Gradually I was able to read lots of different types of children's books and they helped me to improve. Then I thought it was time to move on to grown-up books. My friend Bauza gave me a copy of the thriller *The Shining* by Stephen King but I found it too difficult.

Back home at my apartment in Swansea Marina I would watch the television with subtitles.

In the changing room and after matches I would mix with the other English and Welsh players. It was twenty-four hours a day learning. I would pick up the words they used and if I didn't understand them I would store them in my memory and look them up in my dictionary when I got home. Once I started to understand the meaning of new words and how the phrases worked, I would get excited and want to learn more.

One of my closest friends on the team was Marcos Painter. He was from Birmingham and wanted to learn to speak Spanish, so we helped each other. We would go out together for food and he would teach me words in English and I would tell him the Spanish versions. I made many mistakes along the way. I could tell when I had used the wrong words by the puzzled expressions on people's faces. But I soon got over the embarrassment of being wrong. I told myself, 'Angel, if you are shy you will never learn.' So I kept on trying and as time went by I made fewer mistakes and the words flowed. Eight months after I arrived in Wales, I sat down one night and watched the Sean Penn film *21 Grams* for the first time without subtitles. Within a year I was able to go to the cinema.

On the pitch I began to make a name for myself as a defender playing right back. In training I had been slow at the start because I was unsure of the language.

'Don't swear at the referee or you will be sent off,' my team-mates warned me. So I took their advice and kept my fiery Spanish temper under control. If the referee blew his whistle, I wouldn't speak, I just nodded in agreement.

My first goal came during Swansea's match against Hartlepool. We won 1–0 to go top of the league and I shot from outside the box and scored that winning goal. I felt on top of the world as the fans erupted with cheers. They started to sing my name. 'Angel, Rangel, Angel Rangel,' they chanted. I will always remember how proud I felt at that moment. When my parents visited from Spain, they sat in the crowd and listened to the fans singing my name; it was a proud moment for them, too.

After the match the sports reporters asked me questions about the game and my goal. It was hard for me to answer because my English was not good enough so my friend Bauza became my translator.

During my second year in Swansea I met my Welsh girlfriend, Nicky. Her family live in Mountain Ash in the Valleys and didn't speak a word of Spanish, so soon I was learning Valleys-speak too.

Being with Nicky and her six-year-old son has also helped me. At home we speak a lot of Spanglish, a mixture English and Spanish words, so that my stepson and Nicky can learn Spanish to communicate with my family when we visit them.

We have a baby son, too. Born in October 2010, we named him Angel Rangel. There have been seven generations of my family with the same name, so I upheld the tradition and passed the name on to my son. When he is old enough we will teach him to speak English and Spanish.

Reading books is the easiest way to learn. I am currently reading a book which was given to me by a fan. It's called *King John* and is the autobiography of the great Welsh footballer John Charles, who played for Juventus. When I finish that I will read *Alive and Kicking*, a Quick Read by former Swansea City player Andy Legg about his battle with cancer. But with a new baby in the house, I don't think I will be finding time to finish reading them soon!

In the three years I have been living in Swansea my English has improved. I hardly speak any

Spanish now – except when I call my parents every night to tell them I'm OK. I have also been able to act as translator for some of the newer Spanish players who have joined Swansea.

Sometimes I still get into trouble in interviews with journalists. At the end of the last season Premier League clubs Blackpool and Fulham were interested in signing me, which would have meant leaving Swansea.

Reporters asked me about the possible move. 'It would be a good opportunity for my career,' I replied.

My words were taken out of context and a story ran in the local paper saying that I was disappointed the club wouldn't let me go. I got into a lot of trouble with the club and the fans, who thought I was just in it for the money and my heart wasn't in Swansea. I knew I was in trouble when they stopped chanting my name at matches. When the new season started in September 2010 and I played my first game the crowd sang my name again and I was happy.

I never really plan to go back to Spain. I came here to do what I love and dedicate my whole life to football. I will stay with Swansea for another season until my contract ends, then who knows what will happen? But now

that my English has improved I will not be
afraid to move to a new club.

Building Confidence

by Lord Richard Rogers

'Jump,' the voice in my head said, as I stood in front of the bedroom window looking down to the hard ground below. I was ten years old and feeling desperate.

At that time I did not know I would grow up to become a successful architect. Luckily I didn't jump.

The year was 1943 and I was at boarding school in Surrey, England. I'd been sent there on the eve of the outbreak of World War Two after my mother fell ill with the serious lung disease tuberculosis (TB).

It was a nightmare from day one. At home in Italy I was the youngest child in a traditional, loving Italian family. My father was a doctor. His ancestors were English and he was very passionate about Britain. He bought all his clothes from England and named me Richard instead of the Italian name Ricardo. My mother was a potter by trade and our family was moderately well off. My brother was not born until I was fifteen. I was greatly adored by my

17

parents and grandparents, which made boarding school days even more lonely.

At school I was an Italian in a very English school and at that time, during the war, it was very difficult. I remember having to learn English, which was painful. The other children would laugh at me.

In those days no one had heard of dyslexia, so everyone put my lack of learning down to stupidity. My only aim was to be second to bottom rather than bottom.

I had just one big advantage – I was big for my age and I was a good boxer, so I was able to protect myself. Even today, at the age of seventy-seven I still practise my boxing in my spare time to keep fit. At school I fought my way to the top to become school boxing champion and earned friends and respect from my peers. I had a couple of close friends who supported me and made my school life bearable.

When I was thirteen I changed schools for a year. For me a change was almost as frightening as being beaten and bullied. But my new school was like a miracle. It was a tiny school with only twenty students, and all the children had foreign parents. Being in a small group freed me. Suddenly I became one of their best students. In that one year I caught up by two years and went ahead a further three years. I also got better at sports. One of my teachers was an ex-priest and he gave me some sound advice which helped me to play cricket. 'Don't worry about the style, just hit the bloody ball,' he would say every time I missed. I followed his words and it worked – soon I was hitting fours and sixes.

During that year my reading also improved. I had been a late starter when it came to literacy. Whereas most children in my boarding school were reading at six, I didn't pick up my first book until I was eleven. And then it was a simple 'Cat sat on the mat' type book for young children. At my new school the teachers encouraged me to practise my reading and I got to the point where I was able to read Charles Dickens books like *Oliver Twist* and *Great Expectations*. Although I wasn't as fast as other thirteen-year-olds, I could read any book.

I left that school after a year and went to a public school for boys. And from that point I learnt very little. By the time I left at sixteen my housemaster's report said: 'This boy must leave now and should never go to university or any further education.' He suggested I should join the police and go to South Africa. What he really meant was that because I was a strong boxer I would be able to handle a police baton. At that time South Africans were living under the apartheid system where blacks were forced to live separately from white people and there was a lot of racial tension and violence in the country.

I didn't take the advice of my careers teacher. On leaving school I joined the Army for two years, which was compulsory, as part of the National Service. There I continued to box. But at the end of the two years I still had no idea what I wanted to do with my life. I knew I would never be able to follow in the footsteps of my father and grandfather and become a doctor as I would never be able to sit the exams to get into medical school.

I returned home to Italy where I had a cousin who was a famous architect, designing buildings in Milan and my family's home town of Trieste. And that's when I finally realised what I wanted to do with my life. I wanted to learn how to design buildings. I thought that it would be easier to 'slip in through the back door' with no exams in a creative industry.

But the struggles began all over again when I tried to get into college to study architecture.

I needed 'A' levels. Of course I didn't have any. But my educational records had been lost, so I pretended I had 'A' levels, and I got in to study at the Architectural Association in London.

In the last year of college things dropped into place. I discovered a flair for design and won a scholarship to Yale University in America, one of the world's most famous universities. With the words of my careers master 'You should never go to university' still echoing in my mind, I thought I hadn't done too badly. I was lucky I had parents who never gave up. My mother recovered from her TB while I was still at school and was always supportive of me throughout my childhood. I still had a block in my learning in that I had difficulty remembering names. I could even forget the names of my closest relations, but as I got older I managed to cope by surrounding myself with people who could help me fill in the gaps.

While studying at Yale, I met Norman Foster, a fellow student who was to be very important in my early career. I was never a natural painter and sketcher but Norman could draw extremely well. My talents lay in my ability to work with open spaces, so we made a great team. After university we returned to

London and set up our first architectural business with our wives, Su Brumwell and Wendy Cheeseman. We quickly earned a reputation for our buildings. One of our projects, Skybreak House, which was built in Hertfordshire in 1965, was used in the film *A Clockwork Orange*. Throughout the 70s and 80s I worked with various partners on some of the most exciting building projects of the time, including the Pompidou Centre in Paris and the Lloyd's Building, home of the Lloyd's Insurance company in the city of London.

On 1 March 2006, eight years after my design practice won an international competition to design a home for the National

Assembly for Wales, the Senedd was opened. We had set out to create a building that was open and spacious where the public could view the National Assembly and its members at work. Using Welsh materials like slate and wood, our design made the entire ground floor open and created a debating chamber where the public could look down on politicians. I think I have a good understanding of the design of public spaces and I enjoyed planning the home of the National Assembly.

As I've got older I've learned not to believe people when they say you can't do something – you have to find out for yourself. I was born an optimist and I don't give up. I will continue tugging at problems until I get a result. I've tried not to let my dyslexia hold me back. As well as the Pompidou Centre and the Lloyd's Building, my practice has designed other well-known buildings: the Millennium Dome in London, Terminal 5 at Heathrow Airport, and Terminal 4 at Barajas Airport in Madrid. I am also working on a design for a new tower block, Tower 3, which will be put up on Ground Zero, the site of the Twin Towers in New York.

I've come to accept my weaknesses and know how to work with people who can help. My spelling is pretty appalling. Even the spell check on the computer doesn't always recognise many of the words because they are so badly misspelled. And double letters in words, like 'll' or 'oo', are completely beyond me. Over the years girlfriends have corrected my spelling mistakes. And now my wife Ruthie does the same. Ruthie runs the famous River Café in London which is next door to my architectural practice, Rogers Stirk Harbour and Partners in London. She is one of the most outgoing people I know. She understands my weaknesses and how to help me. When I forget names, she's always there to help. Together we make a pretty good team. Our friends joke that Ruthie and I go everywhere with our arms round each other not because we love each other but so that she can whisper names in my ear. It works most of the time, though sometimes people can get furious if you forget their names. I can't help it, it's the way my mind works. I used to write names on my hand but that became too obvious. My writing is pretty hellish too. My secretary can read my writing better than I can.

I often say that the last third of my life has been much better than the first third. The first twenty years of my life throughout school were mostly a nightmare. But the last twenty years have been a success. I was knighted in 1991 and made a life peer, Lord Rogers of Riverside, in 1996. In 2007 I was named Laureate of the Pritzker Prize for Architecture, the highest international recognition for an architect's work.

I was late discovering my dyslexia. I only realised I had a problem when the first of my five grown-up sons was born. But once you accept you have a problem you can do something about it. I am a strong supporter of dyslexia organisations and the work they do. In my business we employ a hundred and fifty people and a number of them also suffer with dyslexia. I know doctors, lawyers and politicians who are dyslexic but cover it up. They get people to read letters to them because they are ashamed to admit it. That can be tough. It erodes your confidence.

In a way we all have some constraints. We can't all be 100 metres runners and we have to accept our limitations and strengths and try to still have a good life without being able to do certain things. To accept that you need confidence, and that comes from your teachers, your peers, your parents. My advice to any child or young person with a problem is to seek help. Dyslexia can suck out your confidence. I was lucky my parents supported me and I hope – in a way – I have been able to build confidence into the young people I work with.

The Burning Secret

by Joe Monks

The closure of the steelworks in Cardiff was the nightmare event that I had always hoped would never happen. The reason was that I had a secret that I had kept hidden all life, and I was now terrified my secret was about to be exposed.

I was nineteen when I started working in the steel industry. Before that my life had revolved around my job on the butcher's counter at Lipton's supermarket, and Saturday afternoons on the pitch playing for Fairwater Rugby Club. It was the era of Gareth Edwards, JPR and the Pontypool front row, and like every other young man in Wales at the time I had aspirations to play for my country. So when Lipton's wanted me to work Saturdays, I said, 'No way,' and left. At that time nothing was going to get between me and my rugby.

And that's how I found myself walking into the personnel office at Allied Steel and Wire steelworks looking for a job. 'What are you like at fractions?' the manager asked. 'Yeah, great,' I replied and I was telling the truth, my maths was OK. Now, if they had asked me what my spelling or writing was like, that would have been a different story. Then they asked, 'What are you like getting up in the morning?' 'Fine,' I lied, and I was in a job.

'You won't last five minutes son, you can't get up in the morning,' was my father's reaction when I got home and broke the news of my new job to him and Mama. But my father was there to kick me out of bed in the mornings and I lasted the pace.

When I walked into the mill on my first day it frightened the life out of me. The sheer size of the place, the noise from the metal, the searing heat from the furnaces, terrified me. They put me to work in the rod-straightening Torbay Mill. We would take in coils of rod-steel and reprocess them by feeding them through a machine to give them extra strength so they could be used in the construction industry.

It was an intense and sometimes dangerous environment and accidents did happen. Some people would get bits and pieces of their toes and fingers chopped off or mashed up. Other incidents were more serious. During the twenty-five years I worked there I didn't see anyone get killed on my shift, but it did happen. One chap had his head crushed by a fork-lift truck; an electrician was killed because someone turned on the power in the area where he was working. A couple of people fell through the roof to their death. The men working in the steel plant making the steel billets would have some horrible nasty injuries caused by the molten steel.

But it was also a good place to work, with a feeling of togetherness and great sense of humour between the workers. We all had nicknames. I got off lightly with the name 'Monks'. But others were more personal. There was 'Legs Diamond' because he had a funny walk. 'Armpits' had a problem with underarm odour. 'Big Dai' was just big. One guy was called 'Lost in Space', another was 'Waste of Space' and 'Bob the Dog' was the manager. But for all the names and sick jokes, we were good friends and would watch each others' backs. You had to.

It was also an industry that paid well at a time when many of the jobs advertised in the Job Centre would be barely above minimum wage. By the time the works shut down, I had worked my way up to team leader with up to twenty men working on my shift. My salary was £24,500 a year before overtime, and even the basic unskilled workers were earning more than £20,000.

I thought I had a job for life. I was one of the old-timers there with twenty-five years' experience; I knew the machines inside and out. And over the years the workers grew to respect me. I became involved in the union and I earned the respect of the other steel-workers. I had the gift of the gab and could talk to anyone. When the annual pay rise sessions came around I would negotiate with management for the best deal for the workers.

But no one had ever seen me write. I couldn't. My writing and my spelling were shocking. I could stand up in a meeting and argue the reasons why the workers deserved a three per cent pay rise. But put a pen in my hand in public and it felt like squeezing a red-hot poker. It was like being put to stand naked in the middle of Cardiff city centre on a Saturday afternoon; I felt vulnerable.

Even though I had a responsible job as a team leader and had to maintain accident records, time sheets and maintenance log books – no one would ever see me write. If I had any writing to do I would lock myself away in the office and copy other people's writing. However, I couldn't distinguish between right and wrong spelling; as long as it looked all right it would do for me. As soon as I became a team leader I started a training programme where all the men on my shift would learn to do the office and paper work. They would get an increment which meant a couple of quid extra in their pay packet, so they were happy to train up. I ended up with the best-trained shift in the works. If I needed any office work done I would delegate it and check it over later, so I never got found out and my secret remained safe.

Then came the announcement that ASW had gone under and was in receivership, in the weeks that followed the steelworks became the focus for the media and politicians. The eight hundred workers would be out of a job with no redundancy pay. A week later it came to light that the company pension scheme was in deep trouble. It was £21 million in debt and all the workers who had contributed to their pensions all through their working lives would be left without a penny to fall back on in their retirement. The unions launched a campaign. Marches were organised across Cardiff. We even sent a delegation of workers to the Labour Party Conference in Blackpool to lobby support. We marched on Downing Street to meet the then Prime Minister Tony Blair's advisor.

Meanwhile at the steelworks the unions set up the Steel Partnership to help all the men who were facing a life on the dole. Career advisors were on hand to give us advice and funding was put in place to help retrain the redundant workers and get them back into work.

I went into panic mode. My life had been comfortable with my £24,500 a year wage packet. My girlfriend Sian had a job at British Home Stores. We had a mortgage together, credit card bills to pay and had been saving to get married the following year. Suddenly our future looked uncertain.

I wanted to find another job with good pay. But I couldn't walk into the Steel Partnership and say 'I want to train to be a plumber or go to college' as I was too fearful of being exposed. How could I tell people who had looked on me with respect that I could hardly spell or write? I felt as if I had nowhere to turn. I hadn't even told Sian my secret. I was having sleepless nights; I could feel the pressure building day by day and felt as if my head was going to explode. I thought about it long and hard and finally took stock of my situation. Plucking up my courage I walked into the training centre to see the manager.

'I want to train to get back into work but I have a problem that no one knows about. I can't spell and write.' There. It was out in the open, and to my amazement she wasn't shocked or horrified.

'Don't worry, we'll send you to basic skills training and fix up a dyslexic assessment for you,' was her answer. However I wasn't convinced about the basic skills training. I'd been down that path many years ago when I first tried to get help and it had felt as if I was just hitting a brick wall.

My breakthrough came when the Steel Partnership paid for me to have an assessment at the Dyslexia Institute, which I would never have been able to afford myself. I had an in-depth report which found that my reading age was fourteen, which wasn't too bad. My real problems were with spelling and writing. My spelling was like a young child's. They mapped out a learning programme for me.

Driving home that day after my assessment I felt as if a weight had been taken off my shoulders. Deep down I had always felt there was a reason why I couldn't write. It was bad enough growing up being ginger, without saying you couldn't write or spell! But I could read. In school I would try and make my writing bad to cover my bad spelling. People would put me down as a bit dull and I ended up in the bottom stream where no one paid you much attention, especially if you were a bit cheeky as I was.

Even at home I knew I had a massive problem, but no one knew about it. It was my own private nightmare. I never wrote on a birthday card – not even to my mother. I would always ask my brothers or sisters to do it. I was forty-four before I wrote my mother a card because my spelling was so bad. In those days dyslexia assessments were for rich people.

As I turned the corner into my street after my assessment I felt a tear roll down my cheeks. I can't put into words how I felt, knowing that I was finally going to get the help I needed after thirty years. The same day I was offered a job as a security officer at Llandough Hospital, so it was a double reason to celebrate when I went home and broke the news to Sian.

Over the course of the next six years I went from learning my alphabet to graduating from the University of Wales Institute, Cardiff, with a degree in housing policy. I started by enrolling on a three-month intensive course at the Dyslexia Institute (now Dyslexia Action). Most of the other people on the course were dyslexic children, aged from seven to sixteen. At forty-four I was the oldest there by far. It was a really fast learning curve. We did speed tests to get our brains working. We were taught the alphabet by association and I learned to sound my vowels properly. I took it all in and showed promise from the off.

My dyslexic tutor was moving to Cardiff's Coleg Glan Hafren the following year and encouraged me to follow. Within a year I had passed my GCSE in English with a C grade which was a fantastic achievement for me. Every week for the next two years my hours at Coleg Glan Hafren would be spent working with Paula and Pam on my dyslexic problems which was the key to enable me to start achieving academic success. I don't think that I will ever be able to thank them enough or repay them for that help.

I worked hard and gained the respect of my tutors. It was a full-time course, and I was also working full-time at the hospital. I was lucky my employers allowed me to work my shifts around my educational commitments; any spare time I had would be spent on my college work. So I would often finish a night shift at 6 a.m., go home, take the Missus to work, then go to college for a 9 a.m. start. I would work weekends so that I could get time off during the week for classes. It meant that I was having no free time. It was hard but I got through it. In my first year at Coleg Glan Hafren I got my exam results, the equivalent of four GCSEs in sociology, maths, history, geography and an 'A' level pass for poetry. In the second year I enrolled for the Access to Social Work course which would prepare me to study social work at university. It was intense. There were twenty-six students who started the course but only six finished. I passed with flying colours and was nominated for NIACE Dysgu Cymru's Adult Learner of the Year 2005!

I was starting to feel immensely proud of myself, and my confidence was starting to grow. I felt that, as my skills were developing, so my nightmares were disappearing, as if they belonged to some far-distant past. The Access course was equivalent to two 'A' levels, A to C grade, and opened up opportunities to study at university. I was offered places to study criminology and justice at the University of Glamorgan or sociology at Cardiff University but I decided to do housing at the University of Wales Institute, Cardiff (UWIC), as I was told there would be more job prospects in social housing.

After taking some advice I decided to attend university part-time and spent the next four years at UWIC studying Housing Policy and Practice. They were probably the hardest four years of my life but also the most rewarding. In 2006, I passed the Higher National Certificate in Housing Policy and Practice, then in 2007, I was the recipient of the All Wales Chief Housing Executives' Best Housing Student Award at HNC/HND level.

However, 2008 was the year that will stay in my memory for ever. My tutors had seen how hard I was working to overcome my problems with dyslexia, as well as working full time. They were so impressed they nominated me for NIACE Dysgu Cymru's Higher Learner of the Year Award 2008, which I won. Going up on to the stage to collect my award, with all eyes on me, I felt like a celebrity. It reminded me of the days when I was part of the campaign to fight for the steelworkers' pensions and would be interviewed by the TV and newspaper journalists. We'd won that battle too. Most of all I will never forget the look of pride on my mother's face as I was called to the stage to collect my award; it made me feel that I had finally achieved something for the first time in my life.

The award gave me the impetus to go on and finish my degree the following year, something that only a few years before would have been beyond my wildest dreams. Although my time at UWIC was hard, I have to say that it was also a great place to learn; even at my age and with the problems that I had I was made to feel completely at home. The course director, Jane Mudd, was someone you could talk over your problems with when you found the going tough. She was also someone who would give you a kick up the backside if you were slacking, and I have the highest respect for her.

Looking back I feel proud of what I have achieved. When I started out all I wanted to do was to express myself with a pen in my hand. I can write now, although I always print and never use joined-up writing. I'm far better using a computer. When I married Sian in 2004 I wasn't scared when the registrar watched me signing the marriage certificate.

I still spell things incorrectly but I have more confidence. I can write very well now, both academically and descriptively. I'm assistant branch secretary for Unison, and I take notes at meetings. I haven't mastered taking official minutes yet but I'm working on it. I'm also a learning representative for the union and can assess people with basic skills needs and advise them where they can get help; I've helped a lot of people back into education. I'm open about the problems I had and it doesn't embarrass me any more; I often talk openly to people wishing to return to education. I'm living proof that problems can be overcome and that it is not too late for them to realise their own dreams through education.

My journey would have been a lonely and near impossible one without the support of my wife, family and fellow students. As I look to the future, I still have dreams to aim for. I would like to become a local councillor. In the last local elections I stood for Labour in Gabalfa, Cardiff, and I hope to stand in my home patch, Fairwater, next time. I would also like to write my own book one day and even go on to tutor people with basic skills needs. I now know that if I keep working hard perhaps my dreams are not so far away and really might come true!

The Facebook Father

by Edward John

'You're going on holiday today,' my mother said, as she bundled up my clothes and Buzz, my teddy bear, and stuffed them into a Tesco carrier bag.

I was excited. I was six years old and had never been away before, except for the time I was sent to live with my auntie for a couple of months when my alcoholic mother was too ill to look after me. I pictured myself in a caravan beside the sea building sandcastles and going hunting for crabs in rock pools.

But I didn't go on holiday, I went into foster care. A lady in a smart suit and driving a blue Ford Fiesta came to take me away.

We drove for what seemed like ages and eventually stopped outside a nice-looking house in Merthyr. It had a front garden with real flowers and grass, not the bags of rubbish and dog shit that we had in front of our council flat. But I was scared and felt all alone.

'Are you going to come and say hello, Edward?' the smart lady said as she opened the car door. I held tightly onto Buzz. He was only a tatty second-hand teddy, but he was my friend from home. I called him Buzz after Buzz in the film *Toy Story*.

'Hello, Edward. I'm Yvonne, I'm going to look after you while your mother gets better,' said a second lady. She wasn't dressed up like the smart lady. She was wearing jeans and a pink jumper. I thought she looked kind.

'Don't be shy. We've got a nice room for you to sleep in. And this is your new brother, Craig.' An older boy appeared and stood beside the car. He was about nine. He had Nike trainers and an Adidas tracksuit and he looked proper cool, not like me in my worn-out plastic trainers and trousers with holes under my bum.

Yvonne and the smart lady stuck out their hands for me to hold them. And, hugging Buzz, I grabbed Yvonne's hand and she guided me into the posh house and showed me my own room. It was a proper boy's room – a bed shaped like a racing car, bright blue curtains and a pile of games stacked in the corner. The smart lady put my carrier bag of clothes on the bed and went outside onto the landing. 'He's had a hell of a tough life. It will take him time to adjust,' I heard her whisper to the lady called Yvonne.

For the first couple of weeks in foster care, I cried non-stop. I missed the tatty house I called my home, and my mother. I missed the noise of her loud drunken parties, I missed the stale smell of fags and lager. I missed being shouted at.

It took some time but I finally settled into my new home. I forgot about my mother and my old life. Yvonne and her husband Robert were the best parents a kid could ask for. They were kind and generous, they worked hard and lavished us with love and attention. Yvonne worked for the local council and Robert was an aeroplane engineer. They had another foster child called Julia who was eleven and she became my big sister. I was the baby of the family and for that reason I was spoilt.

On our birthdays there were parties and presents, all the latest toys and computer games. Every summer we had holidays, proper holidays. Two weeks in a caravan, just like I had dreamed about. It was wicked.

I was enrolled at a local primary school and for the first couple of years I was a good boy. But when the hormones kicked in during my teenage years, things started to go bad. Whereas I'd loved going to primary school, I hated high school. I lost interest and I fell in with a bad crowd and my school work suffered. 'If you revise you'll get good grades,' my parents would tell me. But I couldn't concentrate on my studies. I wanted to be out with my mates.

'We're going to play football,' my friends would call on their way to the playing field. And I would be right behind them. I didn't have enough willpower to say no and my school work started to suffer. I left school with low grades and went to college to study public services.

I would go to college by day, then out drinking. Most nights I would come home drunk and get violent. I would call my mother all the bitches under the sun and hit my father. I started trashing the house, and then I started running away. In the end social services got involved again and I was told to leave.

I have never seen my mother cry so much as she did on the day she and Robert took me to a hostel for the homeless in Cardiff. The hostel was run by Llamau, a charity for young homeless people. I was given my own room on the ground floor. I hated it. As my parents hugged me and said goodbye, I turned and punched the door. I had gone from having a loving family to being alone. I would bang the walls and smash the windows and get into fights. I was moved to two other hostels and eventually I got my own housing association flat.

That's when I fell in love for the first time. Hayley was her name. She lived round the corner and she was beautiful. She had big brown eyes and gorgeous black curly hair. She looked Spanish, but in fact she was from Bristol.

For the first couple of months, everything was good. We were loved up. We didn't have much money and would spend nights in front of the telly, cwtching together on the sofa watching DVDs.

A year into our relationship things heated up. Hayley was jealous and possessive and would fly into a rage if I spoke to other girls I knew from the hostel. We would argue and fight and she'd lash out at me, leaving scram marks down my face. Then we would kiss and make up.

'I'm pregnant,' she announced one day as we were walking to the garage to buy a pint of milk. I freaked. I was nineteen and she was seventeen and I wasn't sure if we were ready to play happy families. Pregnancy made her even more insane. It was like her hormones were all over the place and the least thing would start her off.

I backed off. Instead of spending all my time at Hayley's flat, I stayed at my own place and we would only see each other at weekends. I told myself, 'In six months you're going to be a father, so pull your finger out and get a job.' I was determined that my baby would have a better start in life than I did, so I began looking for work.

Every week I would be down the Job Centre but as the months went by and the baby's birth got closer I lost hope. I needed to get qualifications that I'd missed out on in school. I needed to improve my maths and writing. So I joined Llamau's Learning4Life centre where I got started on a Basic Skills Level 1 literacy and numeracy course.

My maths was terrible. The only thing I could do was add a few numbers together. My spelling and reading were pretty bad too. With help from my tutors I started to improve my writing and I even learned how to divide numbers. These were things I'd never paid much attention to when I was in school, but I wanted to improve as I needed to find work. I didn't want to be a dole bum all my life.

When I got the phone call telling me I was a father, I was over the moon. A healthy baby girl: 6 lb 12 oz. I rang my foster parents to tell them they were grandparents. Even though I was no longer living with them, we still kept in touch. They always sent me cards and money for my birthday and Christmas. When Hayley first broke the news that she was pregnant, Robert had been the one person I turned to for advice. They were both happy for me.

Later that evening I turned up at the hospital to see my new baby. Hayley's family were sitting around her bed when I walked in and I felt a bit awkward at first. But when I laid eyes on our daughter the bad feelings of the past months disappeared. She was perfect. Thick black hair just like her mother, big blue eyes and tiny little fingers. 'Can I hold her?' I asked nervously as Hayley handed the little bundle in a blanket to me.

From that moment I felt committed to Hayley and our baby, who we named Amy. 'I told you I would be back when the time was right,' I said as I hugged Hayley. But then, soon after she came home from hospital, Hayley started to suffer from post-natal depression and went to stay with her parents, so I took sole care of Amy. She was a real Daddy's Girl. When she cried in the middle of the night, I was the only one there to feed her, change her nappy and nurse her back to sleep. When she woke up early in the morning I would be the one to play with her and make her laugh.

I couldn't carry on my basic skills lessons with a baby to look after, but some days I would take Amy into the centre to see my tutors. They had become friends as well as teachers and I wanted to keep in contact. 'As soon as Hayley's better I'll be back to classes,' I said. 'I want to learn to read, so I can tell bedtime stories to this little one.'

Hayley did get better, but our relationship got worse. The stress of having a toddler started to drive us apart. We tried living together and being a family but it didn't work out.

I returned to Learning4Life and started working on my literacy. I was glad to be out of the house. On my way to class one morning I walked past a charity shop and they had an *In The Night Garden* book in the window for £1. I went in and bought it and showed it to my literacy tutor. We read it together as I wanted to make sure I was able to read it before I took it home. Gradually I moved on to the Quick Reads books. There was a shelf of them in the library at the Learning4Life centre but I'd never bothered to pick one up before. Now I had the reading bug and started off with one of the Doctor Who books. I got into *The Sontaran Games* where the Doctor has to fight a race of ugly monsters with heads like potatoes, before moving onto stories about the Daleks.

One afternoon as I was walking back home from my classes, I saw Hayley's father's silver Ford Focus driving away from Hayley's flat. I knocked on her front door, but there was no reply. The flat was in silence. 'Strange,' I said to myself. 'She didn't tell me she was going out today.' I went back home to my flat and tried calling her mobile. But it kept going to voice mail.

'Where are you? Are you OK?' was the message I left. Eventually a text message came back. 'Gone back to live with mam and dad. Leave me and Amy alone.'

I was gutted. For weeks I went around in a daze. I wanted to hitch a lift to Bristol to find my baby and bring her back home. 'She can't stop you seeing Amy. But give her some time and space and maybe she'll come around,' my Learning4Life tutor advised me. I tried to keep my distance, but it was hard. I tried calling and texting. I wanted to know if Amy was all right.

One day a letter arrived. It looked like it might be from the social or maybe it was a reply to one of the many jobs I'd tried for. It was a legal letter, and it said something about Amy but it was full of big words and I didn't understand what it meant. So I took it to show my support worker at the Learning4Life Centre.

'It's a solicitor's letter that says you can't have access to see Amy,' my support worker explained.

'But I want to see her,' I said. 'What can I do?' I didn't have a clue how courts worked or what my rights were. All I knew was that Amy was my daughter and I wanted to be a good father to her.

Fighting to get access to my daughter has turned out to be a crash course in literacy. My support worker is helping me with all the legal letters, and together we are going through the courts to arrange access. I explain to him the situation and he puts it into writing, I read through the letter and then sign it. At the moment I'm waiting for a court date and hopefully the court will give me the chance to see my baby girl.

Six months have passed since I last saw Amy, but she's growing fast. How do I know? I see her photos on Facebook. Her aunties post pictures from their days out and birthday parties. It's the only way I can keep track of her. Whenever I go on to Facebook there's always a new photo of her for all Hayley's friends to see. It makes me angry that I can't be part of her life.

When the courts finally allow us to be together, Amy will see a new and improved dad. My basic skills lessons have helped me to find a job working on the railway tracks with Network Rail. It's early days, but I hope it'll turn into a job for life.

I have a dream that one day I'll earn enough money to buy myself driving lessons and a car. Then I will be able to pick up my little girl from her mother's house in Bristol, drive her to see her grandparents in Merthyr and we can be a happy family once more.

My Family was Murdered

By Lutala Kabe

A rich businessman once said to me, 'You can never say never – one day you will need to speak English.'

'I will never go to England,' I protested. I had no reason to speak English. I had a well-paid job at one of the largest mineral companies in my home country, the Democratic Republic of the Congo. I was earning up to £200 a month, one hundred times more than the average worker in the Congo, so I was content with my life.

I spoke many languages, including French and Italian and the four national languages of the Congo: Kikongo, Lingala, Tshuluba and Swahili. But I hated English. It all went back to my school days when the English teacher had shouted at me for laughing in class. After that day I detested the language. I threw my books away and said, 'I will never go to a country where they speak English.'

How could I have known that one day my very future would depend on the language I hated so much?

Who could have imagined that war was about to break out in my country? That my family would all be killed and I would be forced to flee more than 6,000 kilometres across the world to seek refuge in the United Kingdom? It was 1992 and in those days my family were happy. We were rich. I was one of sixteen children and we all had good jobs.

Life was good. We lived in a grand house in the capital city of Kinshasa. My family owned farms and factories where we made and sold cheese and chocolate. My mother and father could afford to send me to university to study and when I left I started working as a secretary at the mineral company. Over the years I was promoted. I worked for my family business; I would fly to Paris and Italy trading in gold and diamonds. I married a good man and we had seven children.

In those days my country was beautiful. The third largest country in Africa, its rainforests were home to many species of wildlife, including chimpanzees and gorillas. The many rivers generated electricity and the thriving mining industry produced natural wealth in gold, diamonds and copper. Farmers grew tea, coffee, rubber, cotton, sugar and cocoa on their land which they sold around the world.

But my life and my country would change forever in December 1994 when the civil war in the neighbouring country of Rwanda spilled over into the Congo.

At the time I had left my job to become a Christian preacher. I wanted to use the wealth from my business to help others, so I would travel around the villages preaching the gospel and buying food and medicine for the poor.

On the day in question I was preaching at an Evangelical meeting in the city, when some people came to me and said, 'You should leave because there are people coming to arrest you.'

I didn't think it was a problem. I said to myself, 'I have done nothing wrong, why would they want to arrest me?' But later that afternoon the Rwandese soldiers came and captured me. They threw me in a small house with more than a hundred other women and children where they kept us starved and overcrowded for two weeks. Many women died in that house in conditions so cramped they could not breathe.

From there the Rwandese took me to my father's home which had been burned to the ground. My sister Celine was there with her four-year-old daughter. She was in tears. 'Give us all your money,' the soldiers demanded, with their guns pointed at our heads.

I gave them all the jewellery and money I had. But it wasn't enough – they wanted more.

'You must have more money,' they spat, angry at the thought that we might be hiding money from them. But I had given them everything I owned.

That's when they turned on us. One by one the soldiers gang-raped my niece. She was only four years old, just a baby, and those evil men sexually assaulted her. My sister tried to protect her baby. She ran screaming towards the last man to rape her daughter. As she beat him helplessly with her clenched fist, he pulled out his gun and shot her.

Even now I cannot think about her without crying. She clung to me as her life drained away. Then the soldiers turned on me and beat me with their guns, breaking both my legs. I was left for dead in a pool of blood.

I was lucky that charity workers from the Red Cross found me. They took me to a hospital, then to a safe place on the Ivory Coast. While living there I learned that many members of my family had been killed. I had seven children but only one of my daughters survived and she now lives in America.

During that time my brother was also murdered by the Tutsi rebels from Rwanda who were fighting the opposition Hutu people. He was killed because he had made a videotape showing Hutu people who had come to our country to escape the bloodshed being buried alive by the Tutsi.

The people who killed my brother also tracked me down to my haven on the Ivory Coast. They tortured me, burning my skin with cigarettes and electric wires. They beat me. I still have the scars across my body where they attached the wires to me and gave me electric shocks.

After my brother's death I sank into a deep depression. For six months I was in a dark place and did not want to live. My family had been wiped out. I was all alone and scared that the people who tortured me would kill me like they had murdered my brother.

In desperation I turned to the United Nations Aid organisation for help. They encouraged me to seek refuge in London. I took with me a bag with some of my jewellery, photographs and the manuscript for a religious book I had written in French called The True Light From the Darkness.

When I arrived in Morocco on my way to London I was held by the Immigration Office. I couldn't speak a word of English and could not understand what they were asking of me. I had left the Ivory Coast with the immigration papers that would allow me entry into the country, but when I handed them my passport they said it was fake. They held me for seven nights in a room. I wasn't allowed out of their sight. When I went to the toilet, I had an escort following me. I was frustrated but I couldn't explain. I prayed to God, 'Please don't let me die here.'

My prayers were answered when one of the officers came to check my identity. They had the proof they needed that I was who I said I was. So I was released and allowed to continue my journey to the United Kingdom.

For the first couple of weeks I stayed with my cousin and members of his church. I was well known for my preaching in the Congo, so they were happy for me to stay with them for a short time.

But while I was in London I became very ill. I was suffering from high blood pressure. I went to the nearest doctor's surgery. Unable to speak a word of English I tried to explain that I needed medical help by waving my arms in the air. The receptionist must have thought I was mad and turned me away saying, 'Sorry, the doctor is busy. Go home.'

I did. I went home and took out my English dictionary. I said to myself, 'I will go back to the surgery and this time I will try my best to tell them what is wrong with me.' 'Blood' became the first word I learned in the English language.

I returned to the surgery the next morning and sat in the waiting room. I was determined not to move until I had seen a doctor. Eventually I was given the chance when the buzzer sounded and the receptionist pointed to a door in the corner of the waiting room. Down the corridor I marched, repeating my new English words over and over in my head.

'Blooood. Jump down,' I said to the sandy-haired man in the white coat. He looked at me in surprise. 'Bloood. Jump down,' I tried again. From the puzzled look on his face I knew I was still not making any sense.

I took out my English dictionary and pointed to the words "blood" and "down".

'You are telling me your blood pressure is going down?' the doctor asked and with that he took out a black rubber cuff and fixed it around my arm, pumping it with air until it felt like it would burst. My blood pressure was very high. The doctor laughed and said, 'You are right. Jump, jump, jump.'

'How can I understand your language?' I asked him. He took pity on me, an African woman who could barely walk on two sticks. In addition to prescribing me medicine to reduce my high blood pressure, he also introduced me to a college in London where I could learn English.

Every day I would travel across London. I would wake up at 4 a.m. to get ready and I would get home at 5 p.m. I would sit in class learning new words. I was happy because I was starting to understand English. I said to myself, 'Now is not the time to say I don't like English. I must learn.' I gave it all my heart. And the more I learnt the more I realised that I had made a big mistake when I first arrived in London because I couldn't explain my situation to the Immigration Office.

My English teacher in London encouraged me to return to the Home Office for help. I had nowhere I could call home. Some people in my cousin's church were kind and allowed me to stay with them for one or two nights. I was sleeping on floors and sofas, and some nights when I had nowhere to stay I would end up sleeping on the street.

My teacher said, 'You must go to the Home Office, tell them you have nothing to eat, nowhere to stay.' So I did and the Home Office sent me to a hostel. The hostel was crowded with other refugees from all corners of the world, but it was safe and secure.

After six months they asked me where I would like to be resettled. I looked at the map of Britain and saw the mountains and rivers in Wales and it felt like home. I didn't have any friends or family in Newport. I had never even heard of Wales before, but something about Wales drew me there. I was still suffering from ill health when I arrived in Newport. As the car drove across the Severn Bridge I saw the water of the River Severn, I looked at the green mountains in the distance, and for the first time in many years I felt safe.

I was given a flat and in time my health improved and I was able to return to college. I enrolled on a Skills for Life course and continued to improve my reading and writing in English. Last year I was given an Adult Learner of the Year Award for my efforts and next year I hope to start studying an Access course in Humanities at Caerleon College. Although I can speak twenty-eight different languages including some French and Italian and I have written books in French, English has been the most difficult for me to learn. I don't speak good English even now – I have a problem with some words and grammar and spelling. But I am determined to improve. I have written a book in English called *Kapi the Dog*. It is based on the true story of a dog back home in the Congo. When our villages were being attacked by the rebel armies, Kapi would spin around in circles to alert the villagers that the enemy was coming. He saved the lives of many women and children until he was killed.

I have other stories inside me that I need to write. Millions of people have been killed in my country and women in the Congo are still being raped and beaten. I owe it to myself and women like me to tell our story.

With practice I hope my English will improve. These days I know what the word 'never' means and, like the businessman told me all those years ago: 'You can never say never.'

'Will I Ever Be Able to Read, Miss?'

By Jill Jury

'Jill, the headmistress wants to see you in her office,' Mrs Evans the teacher said, as I collected the children's pencils at the end of another lesson.

Walking along the corridor towards Mrs Jones's door brought a flutter of nerves to my stomach. Here I was, a forty-three-year-old woman with two teenage children, but that feeling of dread at being summoned to the head's office would not go away.

I'd been working as a teaching assistant at my old school, St Bride's Primary School, for four years. Before that I'd been a childminder and then had run the after-school club, but I was still hesitant as I took the familiar trip towards the boss's office.

'Jill Stevens. Go to the headmaster's room. Now!' were the words I could still hear echoing inside my head. When I was a pupil at the school I was known as Jill Stevens, the naughty girl. I was always getting into trouble. I would hit other kids in the playground because they called me 'thick'. Other times I would be frogmarched to see the headmaster because I had been messing around in the classroom. It was my only defence, the only way I knew how to react. I behaved that way out of frustration because, try as hard as I could, I just didn't get the lessons as quickly as the other kids in my class.

Everything was a struggle for me. The other children in my class would tease me because my reading was not as good as theirs. When they were racing ahead reading Enid Blyton books, I was falling behind. I would pronounce words incorrectly. I could never say 'hospital', it always came out wrong as 'hoppital'. 'Hoppital, hoppital,' the other kids would giggle as I walked past and I would react with my fists. It was the only way I could be better than them.

The trip to the headmaster's office became part of my school routine. Every couple of weeks I would sit outside the big wooden door, watching the tropical fish swimming around the school aquarium while I waited to be told off. It was 1969 and in those days a rap across the hand with a ruler was common punishment for bad behaviour.

But this time the journey to the head's office was different. I knew I hadn't done anything wrong. I'd been working hard as a teaching assistant; I was helping the four-year-olds in reception with their alphabet and loved every minute of my job.

'Jill, I'd like to offer you the position of higher level teaching assistant,' Mrs Jones the new headmistress said, with a smile of encouragement. 'It will mean more responsibility, but the school governors and I think you are the ideal person for the job.'

I couldn't believe it. After years of working as a teaching assistant at my old school, I was being offered promotion. Jill, the naughtiest girl in the class, was now going to be Mrs Jury, the higher level teaching assistant. It was hard to believe. When I was a pupil at this school my only ambition had been to get married and be a mother. I only ever wanted to find someone who loved me, get married and have children. I would never have dreamed of working in a school and teaching other people's children.

'You don't have to give me your answer right away,' Mrs Jones said. She must have seen my amazement. 'Go home. Talk to your husband.'

I wasn't sure at first. It was a big step for me. I didn't know if I was ready to take on such a responsible job.

'Go for it!' my husband Steve said when I told him my good news as we sat down to dinner that night. 'You deserve it. You've worked twice as hard as the rest just to get where you are.'

He was right. For the twenty-one years of our marriage he has stood by my side, supporting me through my journey back into learning. He corrected my pronunciation, checked my spelling and read all my essays as I worked towards my degree – a BA Honours in Education. It may have taken me five years, twice as long as some students, but I did it. And when I graduated from Newport College in 2009 with a 2:2, a 'drinking man's degree', Steve was there to watch. How I wished my old school teachers, who had written on my school report 'this is a child who will achieve nothing', had been there to see me in my cap and gown. I finally felt that I made a success of my life. My long years of determination and hard work were finally being rewarded. And being offered promotion in school was all part of that.

A university education was not something that people like me had. I grew up in a council house. Everyone in the village of St Bride's

Major knew the Stevens family. It was hard not to. There were nine of us kids. I was number seven. My dad was a member of the local community council and my mum was a cleaner, so we were well known. But I was always the naughty one. I just wouldn't listen. At primary school some of my kinder teachers would say I was a child with spirit, but it was their way of saying I was a handful. I would do anything to avoid having to sit down and work. I would find reading and writing hard to grasp, and the teachers and other children would make fun of my 'spider writing'. Most of the time I would copy the answers from my best friend, so when the time came to sit the 11 Plus exam, I was lost and I failed dreadfully.

I still remember my final report as I left primary school for secondary school: 'This is a child who will go nowhere. She's achieved nothing in exams. She needs to go to remedial.'

Actually, remedial class wasn't so bad. It was a small class and we got lots of attention from the teacher. I was given work I could do and I started to come first in every subject. For the first time in my life I enjoyed the feeling of success. It was a new experience to me and I loved it. The following year I was moved out of remedial class into the lowest band, the

F-stream. By now I had a lot of gaps in my knowledge and the final four years in school became a struggle. I was constantly being made fun of by the other children because of my poor results. I had very few friends and would try to buy friendship by giving away my sandwiches during the lunch breaks, just so I could be popular for an hour.

All my reports read 'Jill needs to try harder'. I felt I did work hard but literacy and maths were alien to me. Put simply, I didn't understand what was required of me.

When I left comprehensive school at sixteen I scraped six low-grade CSEs but failed maths and English. I needed a job but the thought of filling in an application form filled me with horror and dread. So I borrowed my sister's best suit and went around the shops in Bridgend, knocking on doors asking for work.

At Tesco in Market Street, Bridgend, Mr Jones the manager said: 'I admire your guts, young lady, you can start on Monday.' So I got my first job as a shop assistant stacking shelves at Tesco. I stayed there for seven years. In that time I found someone to love me, Steve, we got married and when I was twenty-five I had my first child, my daughter Rachel. Four years later I had my son Philip. When Rachel started school I realised that I needed help with my own reading and writing so that I could help them with their homework. Till then most of my work at Tesco had been verbal and on the rare occasions I had to write signs for the shelves I would take the work home and practise till I got it right. Thinking I should get an English qualification, I joined Bridgend College. But it was like being back in school and didn't feel right, so I dropped out.

When my children were young, I started working in a local playgroup and as part of the training I studied for a Diploma in Playgroup Practice and a Level 2 qualification in play work. After completing these, a tutor at Bridgend College suggested that if I wanted to progress with my education and complete a child-care qualification then I should attend adult literacy classes.

That's when my return to learning began in earnest. At the age of thirty-three with my own children aged eight and four, I plucked up the courage to walk into a college. This time it was different. There seemed to be more people who were ready to help me improve my reading and writing and I was given assignments that interested me. I sat alongside fifty-year-old men who were desperate to learn to read to their children. I looked around and thought to myself, 'I really must be thick to be here.' It was a terrible way to think and as soon as I started learning I realised that I wasn't thick – and neither were the other people around me. For the first time I was given a letter to write, which gave me a great sense of achievement. Once I had passed my City and Guilds in Word Power, I was able to go back to college to complete my child-care qualification.

Soon I got my first full-time job as a learning assistant at my old school, St Bride's Primary, helping to teach the young children in the reception class to read. I realised that I could make a difference to young children's early education. To help me become a better teaching assistant I enrolled in a Level 3 NNEB child-care course and completed my GCSE in Mathematics and English. Then I enrolled in a five-year part-time Bachelor of Arts in education degree course, course at Brigend College.

In the third year of the degree I started to struggle. The feeling of failure was coming back to me and it was a very stressful time. My tutor was hard on me and would push me to the limits. She would say, 'Are you sure you're up to it?' and that made me more determined to succeed. Around this time I was also tested positively for dyslexia. My struggle in childhood now became clear. So I was given the extra support of a tutor to help me and no longer needed to depend on my long-suffering husband to correct all my work.

With the advice and support of my husband, I accepted the promotion to a higher level teaching assistant. I've been in the job for six years now but that feeling of not being good enough has never left me.

I still find writing daunting and I'm self-conscious about my 'spider writing'. If I can avoid writing notes and cards to people I will or I will use a computer or typewriter. If I have to write a letter to parents I will get my husband to proofread it first for spelling mistakes before taking it to the school secretary.

But I'm not ashamed that I couldn't read when I was there. It's important not to shy away. I was diagnosed with 'Meares-Irlen Syndrome', which means that when I try to read everything jumps out at me. So I have blue and purple coloured overlays to put on the page to help me see words when I read. I also have the same coloured lenses in a pair of my glasses. When I wear my glasses in school, the other children with similar problems feel more at ease.

I've also been given the job of 'intervention co-ordinator', which means I have to look out for the children who are struggling and help them. I understand where they are coming from because I've been in their shoes. Sometimes colleagues will come to me and say, 'Jill we've done the alphabet till we're blue in the face but they're not getting it. What can we do?' I tell them to get big wooden letters of the alphabet and line them up on the floor to make the children walk along them or put the shaped letters in a bag and put a blindfold on the children so they have to feel the shape of each letter. It's all about making letters and words seem like fun.

During the school holidays last summer I had my own homework. I set up a reading record for all the children in the school, which meant I had to type out a list of two thousand books for the children. It took me three weeks but it was something I was determined to do. The local education authority has also invited me to give talks to other teaching assistants. Two years ago I was invited to do a workshop for the Basic Skills Agency based on my degree dissertation on the need for early intervention for maths. It was an amazing moment for me as the conference was attended by primary and secondary school teachers, head teachers and school inspectors, and I was little old Jill Stevens talking to these professionals! It gave me an opportunity to stress the effect that not 'getting it' has on children and why it was important for professionals to understand.

Over the years I have had some amazing comments from the children I have helped and their parents.

'Thank you for helping me and giving me strength in my work. You have helped me so much,' one little girl wrote on a card at the end of the school year. One mother thanked me for 'the energy and passion and enthusiasm' I put into the reading scheme. 'My child has shown such enormous improvement and I am so proud of her,' she said.

Just the other day one ten-year-old boy in my class who is four years behind with his reading looked up to me and said, 'Miss, will I ever get it? Will I ever be able to read?'

I replied: 'Yes, you will, you keep trying and you will be able to get there.' And I know one day he will succeed, just as I have.

Call of Duty

by Jonathan Owen

It was the wrong reason to join the Army, I know, but I thought it would be a laugh. Going out to Afghanistan and fighting for my country seemed better than hanging around north Wales.

I was walking past the Army Careers Office in Bangor one Saturday afternoon in May 2005 when a soldier on a poster caught my eye. He was wearing camouflage, and crawling across the ground with a rifle in his hand. The slogan on the poster said 'Be The Best ... your Army career could start here'.

'You'll never do it. You don't have the discipline,' my granddad said when I went home, full of talk about signing up for the Army and fighting the Taliban.

'You haven't got the patience to spend months in training and having to take orders from other people,' Mam said, even though she knew I was more than capable of sticking up for myself. I had been chucked out of school at thirteen for fighting. Even my friends thought

I wouldn't stick the pace and that only made me more determined.

The following week I went back to the Army Careers office with my mother to make my application. I was excited. At last I had a focus and direction to my life. I had been expelled from high school in Llangefni when I was in the second form. Me and my younger brother were rebels. I used to pay more attention to fighting than I did to learning. I had loads of warnings. The last time, when I threw a chair at my teacher, I was expelled for good.

I didn't care as I hated school, but I loved cars. Mam's boyfriend was a mechanic and at our house we had a garage big enough for eight cars. So he taught me how an engine works. I could strip an engine down and put it back together, no problem. But ask me to work out a long division sum or read a book and I would struggle. The only thing I ever read was *Auto Trader* and *Scrambler* bike magazine. I would get stuck on long words and have to ask my mother for help. My spelling was all over the place, too. I would spell things as I would say them – so nine times out of ten they were wrong.

I realised I had a problem with literacy when I was accepted into the Army and got to

Bassingbourn, near Cambridge, for my basic Army training. I had to sit tests for all sorts of things, to prove I had what it took to be a solider. However, on the numeracy and literacy tests I just scraped by with the minimum pass mark and the Army promised me extra training.

'Well, I didn't expect you to last this long,' my granddad said when I visited him on home leave after my first 14-week training programme.

'The Army life must suit you, you've smartened yourself up,' was my mam's shocked reaction when she saw how much I'd changed. I used to live in hoodies and tracksuits but now I was wearing jeans and jumpers, and cared about my appearance.

From the initial training I was moved to the Infantry Training Centre at Catterick where the job of learning to become a soldier really started. That's where all the new recruits began their careers before joining the infantry and parachute regiments and the Gurkhas. In our group we had boys from all over the country. I made some of my best friends as we pulled together to work through some punishing challenges. The training is designed to break you down and build you back up as a better man. We were taught how to control aggression and we learned how to watch each other's backs and work as a team. If one man wasn't pulling his weight and listening to orders we'd all get pushed further. Training worked for me, I really got into it, and as the weeks passed my fitness level went up until running miles with 55 kgs on my back was no problem.

After eighteen months of training I chose to join the 2nd Royal Welch Regiment as I wanted to show my Welsh pride. I moved to the barracks in Tidworth with another Welsh boy, Ben, who was from Newport. I'd met Ben on the very first day I joined the Army and we'd become best friends.

Two weeks later I was on my way to Iraq. 'You're not going!' my mother cried when I broke the news to her. It was 2007 and more than a hundred soldiers had already been killed in the war there, so she was worried for my safety. But I was a seventeen-year-old soldier and it was the job I had signed up to do.

Out in Iraq my regiment was stationed at Basra Palace. It had been Saddam Hussein's palace until the British troops took over.

When the regiment got there it was the main bombing target for the Iraqi insurgents. I was there for seven months patrolling the palace with the rest of the 2nd Royal Welch Regiment. We were the quick-reaction force on the ground. If anything kicked off we would jump in the tanks and support the other regiments.

To start with I was nervous because I'd heard about the danger from roadside bombs. It turned out that mortar bombs were the worst. The 'Terrys', which was the nickname we had for the Iraqis, would fire the bombs from 2 km away, aiming for the palace. We broke the record for mortar bomb attacks with eighty-four strikes in one week. The bombs would wake you from your beds in the morning. As soon as we heard the warnings we were trained to roll onto the floor and grab our helmets for cover. I can think of better ways of being woken up from bed, but it made your reactions sharp as a knife.

I remember one day after we got back from Iraq I was walking down a street with my friend Ben and we heard a car backfire. We almost shat ourselves as we went to duck for cover! Then we laughed as we realised we were back home. It was funny as hell.

Patrolling Basra Palace with a fully loaded gun in your hand and six hundred rounds on your back was an adrenaline rush. I had been trained to fire a gun on the shooting range at Catterick but nothing could prepare me for the real thing. It was like being in the *Call of Duty* computer game. During our tour in Iraq we lost three men to a roadside bomb. I know that everyone's got to go sometime, but losing a friend makes you realise how fragile life is.

When I got back from Iraq I started thinking about working on my literacy. I knew if I wanted to move up the ranks to corporal or stand a chance of a career on Civvie Street I would have to improve my basic skills. So I went to the Army education office. The education officer put me through an assessment and showed me the weak areas I needed to work on. As I suspected, my literacy and numeracy were poor. They threw me in at the deep end with a crash course for literacy and numeracy, starting with English and maths workshops. Some people take a year to complete the course, and I had only a week! I would attend the education centre from 8.30 in the morning until 4 in the afternoon, practising my maths and spelling and writing. At the end of it I passed my NVQ Level 1 in literacy and numeracy. Moving on to Level 2 was harder, but I stuck at it and passed last November.

At the education centre I got into reading. Apart from my car magazines I'd never been into books, especially ones with twists that left me wondering what was going on. But Quick Reads were short and straightforward and they grabbed me. I liked the *Sun Book of Short Stories* because each story was different. You would read about one thing and move on to something else before you had the chance to get bored. I also read a book by Andy McNab about the war in Afghanistan. I really got into that as I had been out in Afghanistan with the regiment in 2009.

Looking back at my schooldays, I don't think I was designed to go to school. I needed someone to slap me round the head and tell me what I had to do. In a way that's what the Army has done for me. It's given me discipline and a lot of confidence and the education I missed out on. I am twenty now and I don't recognise that cocky teenager who thought fighting the Taliban would be a laugh. The Army has made me a man. When the time is right for me to leave the Army I want to sign up for a resettlement course to learn how to become a plasterer and builder. My long-term plan is to set up in business and to do that I will need to be able to read and write.

Double Trouble

By Ruth Bond

Identical twins. That's me and my sister Rebecca. Born on the same day, 29 September 1989. We look the same, we dress the same, we talk the same. We even finish each other's sentences.

We also have the same illness.

Bipolar disorder is what the doctors call it. Most other people call it manic depression. It's not uncommon. More than half a million people in Britain suffer from it. Even fans of the soap *EastEnders* know what it's like now that Stacey Slater and her mum Jean have the illness. But when you have to live with it in real life it's not like it is on the telly.

'Short hair, short name. Long hair, long name' is how everyone who knew Rebecca and me used to tell us apart. She was six minutes older than me and always wore her hair below her shoulders, whereas I always had a short bob. We grew up with our older sister Katy and our mum. Mum would suffer from bouts of depression and I would end up looking after the home for Mum and my sisters.

Rebecca, or Becca as everyone calls her, was thirteen when she was diagnosed with bipolar. That was seven years ago and back then the condition was not so well known. It was another eighteen months before I was taken into a psychiatric hospital and told that I too had the illness.

People ask what it's like having bipolar and it's hard to put it into words. It can make your mood go from very low, making you feel depressed like there's no hope, to extreme highs when you become manic and your mind races. I was on the higher end of the scale. I would get these thoughts going through my head like my mind was rushing ahead at 90 miles per hour. My sister was at the lower end of the scale and she would get really down, feeling upset and lifeless. When she was having one of her episodes she wouldn't get out of bed or even wash herself.

We were in Year 8 at high school in Cardiff when Becca first started sinking into her dark and depressed moods. Some days Mum and I would have to physically drag her to school. And once there she would refuse to go to her classes.

It was stressful for me. I was thirteen and not very understanding. I had never heard of bipolar disorder in those days and had no sympathy for Becca when she was having what I thought was just another of her sulks. I was being called out of my classes all the time to sit with her, so it meant that my own education was being disrupted and I was falling behind in my studies.

'Pull yourself together!' I would want to shout at her when I saw her sitting in the little room next to the school reception with tears rolling down her face. But I never did. Instead I would try to cheer her up with talk of our favourite TV programmes. '*EastEnders* is on tonight. Do you think Kat Slater and Alfie Moon will get married?' I'd ask. But when she was in one of those moods, nothing would lift her. It was like talking to a wall. All I could do was sit with her and watch her until Mum arrived and took her home – when I could go back to my lessons and try to catch up with what I'd missed.

Mum took Becca to a child psychologist, who diagnosed her bipolar. She was put on tablets to stabilise her mood swings and for a couple of months everything was calm at home. But then I started showing signs of mania.

I was fifteen when I had my first manic episode. At the time I didn't know that's what it was called. To tell the truth, I still don't remember much about it. All I know is that the day started out just like every other day and ended up with me being taken to hospital. Becca and I had gone to school as usual. I'd had a double drama lesson, which was my favourite subject.

At home that evening, things were the same. I cooked tea for me, Becca, Mum and our older sister Katy. I washed the dishes, tidied the kitchen, put a bundle of dirty clothes in the washing machine and sat down to watch *Emmerdale*.

But I couldn't sit still. As the *Emmerdale* music started I jumped off the settee and headed for the front door. 'Where are you going?' Mum called to me as I grabbed my coat.

'I'm going to Chelsea's house. I won't be long.' And I was gone.

I never did get to my friend's house. And when I still had not returned home hours later, Mum called the police. They found me wandering the streets on the outskirts of Cardiff – four miles away from my home.

What's going on? Why am I here? I haven't done anything wrong, I thought when I saw the car with the flashing blue light pull up alongside me as I was walking along the pavement.

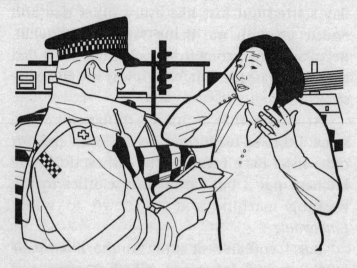

'Ruth Bond?' the policeman asked. 'You're coming home with us.'

When I got home Mum took me to hospital where they gave me some tablets. 'They should knock her out for a couple of days,' the doctor said, handing Mum a prescription for sedatives.

They didn't and the next morning I was still climbing the walls. So Mum took me back to the psychiatric hospital and there I stayed for six months. It was good in hospital. I was on a wing with other young people, some younger, some older. One girl had bulimia, another had anorexia. We all had our own private rooms.

As the months passed and my condition became more stable the hospital allowed me to go outside. At first my family would visit me and we would go walking around the hospital gardens, talking about what we'd been doing and the programmes we'd watched on telly. Sometimes my dad and his girlfriend would visit and take me out for a drive in the car. Eventually I was allowed to go home for weekends.

During my time in hospital I started to catch up on my reading. 'Reading will help to calm you and bring you down to a steady level,' the doctors said. They were right.

I'd never been interested in books when I was younger. We were more of an active family – gymnastics club, drama groups, dance classes and pantomimes at Christmas. My dad was the producer of the local amateur operatic society so we would get involved whenever we could. We never had books at home and the only time I read a book was in school. I never read for pleasure and would find some books difficult to follow. I once tried to read a book which was written in a diary style. I can't remember what it was called, but it was confusing and I couldn't follow it. The story kept jumping around and in the end I couldn't be bothered and put it down. I liked books that were simple to read.

In hospital for the first time ever I started to read the Jacqueline Wilson children's books that I missed out on in primary school. I would get lost in the world of Tracy Beaker and her adventures in the children's home. I loved *Double Act*, the story of identical twins Ruby and Garnet who did everything together. It was just like Becca and me when we were little. Gradually, as my reading got better, I moved on to books for older teenagers.

After six months in hospital I was finally allowed to go back home. I was scared because I knew that I would have to go back to school and it worried me. Some of the kids would tease Rebecca saying, 'Your sister's in a mental institute', so I was frightened that I would get called names too.

I had to go back to school as in a few weeks the GCSE exams would start and I didn't want to miss out and leave school with no qualifications. I gradually worked my way back into school life, starting with just a couple of hours a day, but I had a lot to catch up on. I'm pleased to say all my old friends stuck by me. If anything was said about my mental state, I didn't hear it.

After all I'd been through, I was proud that I managed to sit all but two of my exams. All my grades were lower than Cs, but at least I passed and it was enough to get a place in college to study health and social care.

However, learning how to wipe bottoms and dress old people wasn't really for me. I wanted to work with children. I was babysitting for my friends regularly and wanted to make a career of it, so I signed up for an NVQ in child care at a local training centre. It went well at first but towards the end of the course I began to struggle with work experience placements and dropped out before I finished the course.

While I was at college life at home started to deteriorate. My sister and I would start arguing, tensions would rise and my mother couldn't cope with the two of us and our mood swings. It seemed that if I was all right Becca would be unsteady and vice versa. 'You should think about getting a place of your own,' Mum suggested and introduced us to the homeless and women's housing charity Llamau, which helped us both on to the housing ladder. We now have our own council flats – and miles apart, so we can't argue.

Through Llamau I was able to catch up on the basic skills literacy and maths I'd missed during my last year of school. The tutors at Llamau's Learning4Life centre eased me back into education. I joined their basic skills literacy and numeracy programme, where I learnt things that I was never taught in school. Working in a small group I was taught different tips and techniques, new word patterns and simple sentence structures and my spelling and writing improved. I now have a much better grasp of English. I've enrolled on a Learn Direct course to improve my English grades and I'm working towards my Level 2 Literacy.

Learning4Life has boosted my confidence and given me lots of opportunities. Last year before the General Election I was interviewed by a journalist from a national newspaper and the video they filmed ended up on YouTube. I also met the comedian Eddie Izzard, when he popped into the centre before his show at Cardiff International Arena last year. I was later told that he had reading problems because of dyslexia.

In the library at the Centre I first discovered Quick Reads books and they got me hooked. Some days I would just sit in the corner of the centre, totally in my own world, with my head in a Quick Reads book. These books were easy to get into, not like the books I'd tried to read in the past. I read Hayley Long's *Vinyl Demand* and moved on to *A Day to Remember* by Fiona Phillips. Once I got into them I couldn't put them down and would read them in one sitting. After reading those I got into other books; celebrity biographies and true stories are my favourite. I've just finished reading Cheryl Cole's biography, which I really enjoyed. Quick Reads have helped me enjoy reading for pleasure.

On World Book Day last March the Welsh Books Council invited me and a group of students from Llamau to go down to the Welsh Assembly in Cardiff Bay to receive a hamper of Quick Read books. We met the TV presenter Lucy Owen and Assembly Member Leighton Andrews, who presented us with lots of new books to read. It was great being back as it reminded me of my work experience where I got to work in the press office with Kirsty Williams AM and had the chance to spend a week monitoring the newspapers and writing news summaries. That's something I would never have dreamed of doing before I joined Learning4Life. I've even stood up at an education conference in Swansea run by the

Funky Dragon Children and Young People's Assembly for Wales. There I spoke to potential school leavers and young people who had left school with no qualifications about my experience at Learning4Life and my new journey back to education and training. 'The journey never stops, even when you leave school,' I explained to them.

My reading and writing have definitely improved and I'm confident filling out job applications now. I did my first cover letter for a job application to Ikea. I got an interview, but I didn't get the job. I still hope to complete my National Vocational Qualification in child care and work in a nursery. My tutors think I would make a good teaching assistant. They say I'm very nurturing with a big heart. I suppose I am as I do like helping the newer students.

I'm still on medication for my condition, but the dose has been dropped to just one tablet a day. People ask me how I cope with my illness and I tell them, 'All you can do is get on with life and make the best of opportunities when they come.' That's my motto.

10 of the World's Most Successful Dyslexics

Richard Branson
British billionaire and founder of the Virgin group of companies, which includes Virgin Records and Virgin Atlantic airline, he is ranked among the top 300 wealthy people in the world.

Agatha Christie
The most successful mystery writer of all time, who created the famous detectives Hercule Poirot and Miss Marple, had problems with spelling.

Tom Cruise
One of Hollywood's most successful actors and star of many films including *Top Gun*, *Mission: Impossible* and *The Last Samurai*.

Leonardo da Vinci
The Italian artist, famous for painting *The Mona Lisa* and *The Last Supper*, is considered to be one of the greatest painters of all time.

Muhammad Ali
The three-times heavyweight world boxing champion is ranked among the greatest boxers in the world.

Steve Jobs
The American businessman and inventor is best known for being the co-founder of Apple.

Keira Knightley
One of the highest-paid English actresses in Hollywood, she starred in films like *Bend It Like Beckham* and *Pirates of the Caribbean*.

Jamie Oliver
The British chef is famous for his *The Naked Chef* TV series and books and his campaign to get British school children to eat healthy food.

Steven Spielberg
The Oscar-winning director is one of the richest in Hollywood. Films like *Star Wars*, *Jaws*, *E.T. the Extra-Terrestrial* and *Jurassic Park* broke box office records when they were released.

Thomas Edison
The American inventor, scientist, and business-man who invented the light bulb and many other important devices including the phonograph and the motion picture camera.

Literacy in Wales
in Numbers

- **25** per cent of the Welsh adult population (440,000 people aged 16–65) have levels of literacy below Entry Level 1 – the standard of 11 to 14-year-old GCSE grade D–G students.
- Almost **4** out of every **10** adults in Wales over the age of 16 have reading levels at Entry Level 1.
- A further **4** of out **10** people in Wales have Level 2 reading skills equivalent to 16–18-year-old GCSE grade A–C students.
- **9** out of 10 readers prefer real life stories.
- **1** in 5 adults using Quick Reads got a better job since using the books.
- More than **50** per cent of adults using Quick Reads said their job prospects had improved since reading the books.

Based on statistics supplied by Basic Skills Cymru

Famous last words...

'Scrabble was invented by Nazis to piss off kids with dyslexia. The word dyslexia was invented by Nazis to piss off kids with dyslexia.

What's the point in coming up with a word like dyslexia to explain a word blindness spelling problem ...
Just call it bonk.'

Dyslexic stand-up comedian and actor Eddie Izzard, who spent part of his childhood in Skewen and attended St John's Boarding School in Porthcawl.